FREEDOM OF WORSHIP

By
Victoria Sherrow

THE MILLBROOK PRESS
Brookfield, Connecticut

Published by The Millbrook Press, Inc.
2 Old New Milford Road
Brookfield, CT 06804
© 1997 Blackbirch Graphics, Inc.

5 4 3 2 1

Created and produced in association with Blackbirch Graphics.
Series Editor: Tanya Lee Stone
Editor: Lisa Clyde Nielsen
Associate Editor: Elizabeth M. Taylor
Production Editor: Laura Specht Patchkofsky

Photo credits
Cover and page 6: Photodisk; pp. 5, 26: ©Blackbirch Press, Inc.; pp. 9, 25,
38: AP/Wide World Photos; pp. 11, 12, 14, 16, 17, 23: North Wind Picture
Archives; p. 18: National Portrait Gallery; p. 19: Library of Congress;
p. 22: ©Tom Croke/Liaison International; pp. 29, 30: National
Geographic/Collection of the Supreme Court of the United States; p. 31:
©Steve Liss/Gamma Liaison; p. 32: Brown Brothers; p. 33: National Park
Service/Nez Percé National Historical Park; p. 35: ©Donna Bise/Gamma
Liaison; p. 40: ©Tom Smart/Gamma Liaison.

Library of Congress Cataloging-in-Publication Data

Sherrow, Victoria.
Freedom of worship / Victoria Sherrow.
p. cm. — (Land of the free)
Includes bibliographical references and index.
Summary: Explores freedom of worship, as guaranteed by the Bill
of Rights, along with its history and importance to the formation of
the United States of America.
ISBN 0-7613-0065-1
1. Freedom of religion—United States—Juvenile literature. 2.
United States—Religion—Juvenile literature. [1. Freedom of
religion.] I. Title. II. Series: Land of the free (Brookfield, Conn.)
BR516.S477 1997
323.44'2'0973—dc20
96-21962 CIP AC

Contents

★ ★ ★ ★ ★ ★

Introduction

★ ★ ★ ★ ★ ★ ★ ★ ★ ★

Suppose that you could be arrested for reading a book, going to church, or talking with your friends. Sound impossible? Not everywhere. Your rights to do all these things, and many others, are guaranteed under U.S. law. But people in many other countries have no such guarantees. Their governments tell them what they may and may not read, write, and say, what religion they must follow, and even how they should vote—that is, if they are allowed to vote at all.

Americans are proud of their freedoms. Even so, many Americans don't know very much about those freedoms, or about the responsibilities that come with them. It is important to understand your rights, so that you can use them—and defend them.

The books in the *Land of the Free* series tell you about our most important American rights and freedoms: the right to speak freely, to vote in elections, to worship as we choose, and to join with others who share our views and goals. Most of these rights are set out in the U.S. Constitution and its first ten amendments, the Bill of Rights.

The Constitution and the Bill of Rights were written more than 200 years ago, soon after the United States won its independence from Britain. The authors of the Constitution believed that freedom would flourish under democracy. A democratic government, elected by the people, serves the people—not the other way around. Many of the rights in the Constitution help guarantee that democracy will continue.

The authors of the Constitution broke new ground, creating a society that valued and respected liberty. Over the years, adapting to changes in society, Americans have re-interpreted and expanded the rights that the country's founders set out. Yet, the basic principles behind those rights have not changed, and they apply just as well today as they did 200 years ago. Only if we understand how our freedoms work, and why they are essential, will they continue to flourish for years to come.

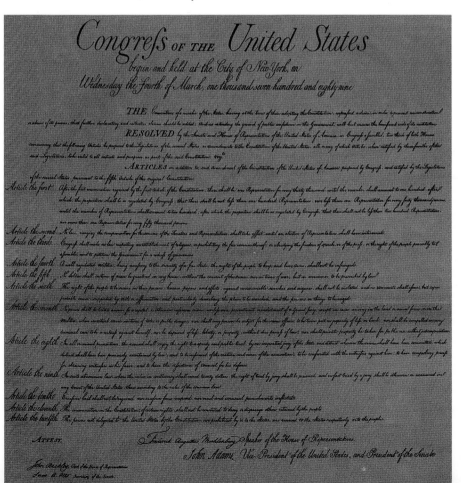

• The freedom to worship is one of the
fundamental rights granted in our Constitution.

FIRST IN THE BILL OF RIGHTS

Visitors to the United States are often amazed by the number of different religions Americans belong to. Across the nation, people can be seen worshiping—paying respect or honor to their God—in various ways. They may worship at churches, synagogues, mosques, temples, or meeting houses, each according to his or her religion. They may worship on Sundays, Saturdays, Fridays, or on other days.

Still other Americans follow no organized, or formal, religion. Under the Constitution, people in America are free to believe in the religion of their choice, or in none at all.

A Revolutionary Idea

When the United States was formed in the late 1770s, the idea that a country could promise religious liberty to its citizens was completely new. Most settlers had suffered from religious persecution in their homeland, that is, they had been treated cruelly for their religious beliefs.

The men who wrote the U.S. Constitution and Bill of Rights wanted to protect individual freedoms. They imagined a nation governed by the people themselves, rather than by a king or by a religious leader or organization. In order to form what they called "a more perfect union," these men designed a democratic system in which citizens would have certain rights that the government could never take away.

One of these rights was freedom of religious worship, stated in the First Amendment of the Bill of Rights. This same amendment that grants freedom of worship also guarantees freedom of speech and freedom of the press.

The Religion Clauses

Religious liberty was the first freedom listed in the Bill of Rights. It is stated at the beginning of the First Amendment in these words:

Congress shall make no law respecting an establishment of religion or prohibiting the free exercise thereof....

These 16 words are called the Religion Clauses of the First Amendment. The first 10 words, or clause, called the Establishment Clause, forbid the government from establishing—setting up or sponsoring—any particular religion.

The second clause of the amendment is called the Free Exercise clause. It says that the government cannot make any laws "prohibiting the free exercise" of religion. In other words, the government may not stop people from practicing their religion, unless their actions violate the rights of other people.

Interpreting the Law

How does the First Amendment guarantee of religious freedom operate in our daily lives? The U.S. Supreme Court is the nation's final authority in interpreting the Constitution. In one famous 1947 case, the Supreme Court summed up important aspects of freedom of religion. Writing for the Court, Justice Hugo Black said,

Supreme Court Justice Hugo Black wrote a landmark opinion in 1947 that prohibited government from interfering with religion.

Neither a state nor the Federal Government can set up a church. Neither can pass laws which aid one religion, aid all religions, or prefer one religion over another. Neither can force nor influence a person to go to or to remain away from church against his will or force him to profess a belief or disbelief in any religion. No person can be punished for entertaining or professing religious beliefs or disbeliefs, for church attendance or non-attendance.

We can see how these ideas operate in our daily lives. In America, we cannot be arrested for having certain religious beliefs—or for having none at all. No matter what our religious beliefs, all citizens have the same rights—for example, to vote, run for public office, attend school, marry, obtain a job, start a business, or follow a profession. No government official can take away these rights.

Freedom to worship means that we may pray or perform other religious activities when we wish, as long as we do not disrupt others. Young people may pray, for example, on their own, at school. A group of students may also pray at recess or lunchtime as long as such prayers are voluntary and do not interrupt school activities. The Constitution, however, forbids the government from taking sides in religious matters. So, since public schools are run by the government, the schools may not force students to pray. They may not favor one religion over another, nor may they sponsor—support or take responsibility for—religious ceremonies of any kind.

A Balancing of Rights

The Religion Clauses of the First Amendment work in careful balance to guarantee religious freedom. On the one hand, they forbid the government from telling people how, why, or when to worship. The Religion Clauses leave those decisions to each individual.

They also protect individuals from tyranny (unfair rule) by the majority. This means that people who belong to a majority group may not practice their religion in ways that limit the freedoms of those in the minority. Americans need not support religion through words, deeds, or taxes, unless they choose to do so. The majority religion may not use government power or public forums to promote its own ideas and practices.

A Nation Where Religion Thrives

In 1831, a French writer named Alexis de Tocqueville toured the United States. He wanted to see how Americans lived and how they put principles of freedom into action. In his famous book *Democracy in America*, de Tocqueville wrote that he was quite impressed by "the religious atmosphere of the country." He said that in France, in contrast, the spirits of religion and freedom had tended to march in "opposite directions."

De Tocqueville discussed this subject with many Americans. He became convinced that the separation between government and religion in America had caused religion to flourish.

Religious freedom continues to thrive in the United States. Today, hundreds of different religious groups exist in the country. Americans have high rates of membership in religious organizations, attend worship services in great numbers, and contribute generous sums of money to support religious institutions.

In more than 200 years, there has never been a religious war in America.

Alexis de Tocqueville

Protecting Freedom of Worship

America's religious freedom did not come easily. It is a precious heritage, one of our basic rights. But with rights come responsibilities. To meet those responsibilities, we must understand how and why the freedom to worship developed and learn how to protect it.

• America's earliest European settlers came to this land in search of
religious tolerance and freedom to worship as they pleased.

Chapter 2

THEY CAME FOR FREEDOM

The story of freedom of worship in America begins years before the Bill of Rights was written. The Europeans who colonized North America, and the immigrants from many lands who came later, sought freedom to live as they saw fit. Often, their chief reason for journeying to the strange new land was to enjoy freedom of religion.

Centuries of Intolerance

Most American colonists came from European countries where government and religion had been closely connected for centuries. Often, rulers received some of their authority from the official religious body. Religious leaders had political and economic power. As a result, many governments were intolerant of—they did not permit or accept—religious differences.

Religious intolerance dates back thousands of years. Rulers in ancient Egypt, Israel, and the Roman Empire forced people to follow the official, or state, religion. Jews and early Christians who refused to obey were most often persecuted. Jews in particular were persecuted both in ancient times and in modern Europe, after Christianity became the main religion.

During the Middle Ages (from A.D. 400 to 1400), some rulers persecuted non-Christians and others who questioned the official church. Heresy—speaking out against religious teachings—was a crime. People who committed heresy or who spoke disrespectfully about the official religion might be fined, beaten, imprisoned, or exiled—sent out of the land. Some were tortured, or even killed. People might also be punished for not attending church services or for failing to pay taxes to the official church.

At times, religious wars were fought between governments or between groups of people. These kinds of wars have been among the most bitter in history. Many conquerors tried to force their beliefs on those whom they defeated.

In ancient Rome, people who did not follow the official state religion were punished or killed.

During these earlier times, members of a certain religion might be allowed to worship freely, or they might not. Freedom to worship was not guaranteed in any way: That freedom could be granted, limited, or even completely taken away.

Religious Variety in the Colonies

One of the most familiar stories in American history is that of the English Pilgrims who arrived on the shores of Cape Cod, in present-day Massachusetts, in 1620. These men, women, and children called themselves Separatists. They had separated from the official Church of England in order to worship in their own way.

Other groups also made their way to American shores. The Puritans, who had also left the Church of England, founded the Massachusetts Bay Colony during the 1620s. What is now New York State became home to people of the Dutch Reformed, Catholic, Anglican, Quaker, Baptist, Lutheran, Presbyterian, and Jewish faiths. Members of these groups settled in the Mid-Atlantic and Southern Colonies. Catholics, disliked in some places, were welcomed in Maryland, which had been founded by Lord Baltimore, himself a Roman Catholic from England.

The colonies grew more varied as Methodists, Moravians, Anabaptists, French Huguenots, and people of other religions from a variety of countries arrived. Some groups, like the Austrian Salzburgers and the Italian Waldensians, had just a few dozen members. Larger groups numbered in the thousands. In this new land, all hoped to worship freely.

From Old Ways to New

Many of the colonists came from lands where religious intolerance was common. Some brought old prejudices and customs with them to North America. At times, majority groups oppressed the minority. The majority Protestants, for example, passed laws that discriminated against the minority Catholics. And the Puritans of Massachusetts refused to let members of other religious faiths vote. Several other colonies named an official church and required all citizens to support it with their taxes.

Other colonies were more accepting of different religions. In Flushing, Long Island, it was illegal to condemn, punish, or banish a person because of religion. In 1649, the colony of Maryland passed the Act of Toleration. This law made it illegal to insult people for their religious beliefs or to call them insulting names.

William Penn founded the colony of Pennsylvania on the principles of tolerance and freedom for all religions.

When William Penn, a Quaker, founded Pennsylvania, he invited people of various religions to live there. By 1776, there were about 400 different religious groups in Pennsylvania, making it the most religiously diverse colony. There, friendship and goodwill developed among people of different faiths. During the Revolutionary War (1776–1783), some non-Jewish citizens of Philadelphia helped to build Mikveh Israel Synagogue. Later, members of that synagogue generously gave land for a Protestant church.

The Religious Freedom Experiment

Although clergyman Roger Williams was deeply religious, Puritan leaders in the Massachusetts Bay Colony accused him of heresy. Williams had said that governments should not push people toward certain beliefs. "Forced worship is false worship," he said. People must be free to seek truth and question religion in order to find God, he believed. Williams also visualized a "hedge or wall of separation between the garden of the church and the wilderness of the world."

Because of his "dangerous opinions," Roger Williams was cast out of the Massachusetts Bay Colony in 1635.

Wampanoag Indians helped him find his way south of Cape Cod, where some Narragansett Indians gave him land. There, Williams founded his colony of Rhode Island. He invited people of all religions to take part in what he called a "lively experiment." Native Americans there also enjoyed religious and political freedom. The colony's charter—the document that established the colony—said that nobody could be punished, disturbed, or questioned "for any differences in opinion in matters of religion." Rhode Island showed that a colony that permitted religious differences could survive.

After being expelled from the Massachusetts Bay Colony, Roger Williams founded a more tolerant community in Rhode Island.

During these years, Americans were examining the old ways and discussing new ways to be free. Colonial leaders declared that people were born with certain rights that no government should be able to take away. No longer should they consent to be ruled by kings. Americans, they said, should govern themselves, guided by a written Constitution.

The Founders of America planned a system of government that guaranteed religious freedom. Written in 1787, the U.S. Constitution gives the government no power in the area of religion. Article VI forbids the use of any religious tests in qualifying people for public office. A few years later, the Bill of Rights strengthened even more individual religious freedoms.

Bill of Rights author James Madison was a strong advocate of religious freedom in America.

A Written Guarantee

Several early statesmen strongly influenced the First Amendment. Thomas Jefferson was proud to have written the Virginia Statute for Religious Freedom. In 1786, it made Virginia the first state to grant full religious equality. Jefferson believed that individual rights should be listed and added to the Constitution. George Mason of Virginia was among the others who had asked for a Bill of Rights at the original Constitutional Convention. James Madison promised that he would submit one.

Thomas Jefferson's "Wall of Separation"

Thomas Jefferson, a champion of religious liberty, liked to imagine a "wall of separation" between government and religion. The idea of such a wall dates back to colonial days, when the nation's founders sought ways to protect freedom of worship. Roger Williams used the words "hedge or wall of separation" in the 1600s. Later, Thomas Jefferson used this symbol in a famous letter.

In 1801, President Jefferson received a message from the Danbury Baptist Association in Connecticut. It said,

"Our Sentiments are uniformly on the side of Religious Liberty—That Religion is at all times and places a Matter between God and Individuals—That no man ought to suffer in Name, person or effects on account of his religious Opinions—That the legitimate Power of civil Government extends no further than to punish the man *who works ill to his neighbors.*"

In his reply, Jefferson wrote, "Religion is a matter which lies solely between Man & his God." He said that nobody should have to account to others for his or her faith or style of worship and that the powers of a government should "reach actions only, and not opinions." In closing, Jefferson praised Americans for having erected "a wall of separation between Church and State." This phrase is still used today to describe the American system.

Thomas Jefferson championed the idea of "separation between Church and State."

Arriving in Congress in 1789, Madison submitted his Bill of Rights. He had based his amendments partly on the Virginia Declaration of Rights. That document said, "All men are equally entitled to the free exercise of religion." Madison had written, "No State shall infringe the equal rights of conscience...."

Four years earlier, Madison had successfully fought a plan to use taxes to support a variety of religious institutions in Virginia. He argued that if a government had the power to support one religion above others, then the majority might deny freedom of worship to the minority.

Members of Congress discussed several different ways to write the First Amendment. Samuel Livermore of New Hampshire suggested this wording: "Congress shall make no laws touching Religion, or infringing the rights of Conscience." Madison objected when some leaders wanted to use the word "toleration." Toleration, he felt, suggests that one view is the right view, and others are merely allowed to exist along with it. Madison said, "The right of every man is liberty, not toleration."

After much debate, the First Amendment was written:

Congress shall make no law respecting an establishment of religion, or prohibiting the free exercise thereof; or abridging the freedom of speech, or of the press; or the right of the people peaceably to assemble, and to petition the government for a redress of grievances.

By 1791, a majority of states had approved the Bill of Rights. For the first time in history, people had a written promise of religious freedom.

Conflicts over Religion

The Bill of Rights did not make full religious freedom a reality for everyone in America. Some laws, left over from colonial days, denied rights to certain people, usually non-Protestants. Until 1844 in New Jersey, for example, only Protestants had full civil rights. Until 1868, taxes paid by Connecticut citizens helped to support Congregational churches. New Hampshire did not let Jews or Catholics hold public office until 1876. That same year, Jews in Maryland were finally allowed to vote. A Massachusetts law said that a person could be put to death for speaking disrespectfully about God. Some laws like these remained until the 1900s.

The rights of Native Americans had not been recognized at all in the Constitution. Many whites thought that Indians should convert (change) to Christianity. Native Americans were often forced to join and work at missions, where they were taught Christianity.

Some Americans feared or mistrusted others who were different, and because of this, certain religious groups were persecuted. One such group was the United Society of Believers in Christ's Second Appearing. Its members called themselves Believers. Others called them Shakers because they often trembled during prayers.

A Shaker group led by Ann Lee came from England to America in 1774. By the early 1800s, about 6,000 Shakers lived in New England as well as New York, Ohio, and Kentucky. In many places, people tried to force them out. In her diary, Molly Goodrich wrote in 1810 that an armed mob of more than 600 men had demanded that

Jews Find a Haven in Early America

Touro Synagogue, founded in Newport, Rhode Island, in 1763, is the oldest synagogue in the United States.

Jews have a history of persecution that goes back thousands of years. In the past, they were forced to live apart from others and were denied jobs, educational opportunities, and basic civil rights. Often, they were the targets of violence.

In 1492, a royal decree expelled Jews from Spain. Many were killed; others were ordered to become Christians. Some Jews moved to Spanish colonies in South America, but they were not treated much better there. Twenty-three Jews from Brazil founded the first Jewish community in North America, in 1654, in New Amsterdam (now New York). But Governor Peter Stuyvesant forbid them to build a synagogue of their own.

Other Jewish people went to Rhode Island in search of religious freedom. There, they were able to worship without fear in the first American colony to have no official church. Jews settled in Newport, Rhode Island, in 1658. They soon developed the second-largest Jewish community in North America and built Touro Synagogue in 1763. The stark and simple building still stands today as America's oldest Jewish house of worship.

When President George Washington visited Newport in 1790—the year after his inauguration—he was warmly welcomed by Jewish citizens. The congregation at Jeshuat Israel wrote to him, praising the new government for granting people "liberty of conscience" and all the rights of citizenship. They praised Washington for leading a nation that would not allow persecution.

Washington wrote back, saying, "All possess alike liberty of conscience and immunities of citizenship." Near the end of his letter, he said, "May the Children of the Stock of Abraham, who dwell in this land, continue to merit and enjoy the good will of the other inhabitants, while every one shall sit in safety...and there shall be none to make him afraid."

her Shaker community give up their faith or leave the region. States tried to pass laws limiting Shakers' rights, but some courts struck down these laws. In the 1830s a New Hampshire court protected the Shakers, saying, "We cannot try the question of which religion, theirs or ours, is the better one.... Theirs is equally under the protection of the law, as ours."

A large Shaker gathering at a meetinghouse in New Lebanon, New York.

The Nativist Movement

More immigrants came to America during the 1800s. Most were poor and uneducated. They competed for unskilled jobs and often were willing to work for lower wages than native-born people. Some Americans blamed immigrants for a rise in poverty, crime, and disease. And, they did not always like the newcomers' religions.

Anti-Catholic feelings were expressed during this time, often toward immigrants from Ireland. Anti-Catholic riots broke out in Boston, Philadelphia, and other cities. Citizens hostile toward Catholics also formed a political party called the Nativists. Groups of Nativists tried to limit the newcomers' rights, such as voting. They feared a majority of Catholics might elect people who favored their own religious causes.

The Nativist movement lasted into the 1900s, fueled by anti-Catholic writings. In response, Catholic leaders spoke out in favor of religious freedom for all, with separation between church and state.

Catholics were not the only target of the Nativist movement. More Jews came to America during the 1800s and 1900s, fleeing from religious persecution in Europe and Russia. They, like Catholics, were discriminated against and treated badly in some parts of America. In many places, Jews were kept out of certain jobs, schools, colleges, and clubs.

During the Civil War, some citizens and members of Congress tried to add a "Christian amendment" to the Constitution. This amendment stated that the United States was a "Christian nation." It did not receive enough support to become law.

New Religions Seek Protection

Meanwhile, new religious groups had developed on American soil. Mormons—members of the Church of Jesus Christ of Latter-Day Saints—settled in Utah. Until 1897, the Mormon religion allowed men to marry more than one woman. This practice upset many Americans. They urged their state officials to pass laws forbidding Mormons from voting. Some states seized Mormon property. Angry citizens attacked Mormon communities.

Members of some religions were criticized when they refused to take part in military service. Quakers, Amish, Mennonites, Brethren, and Moravians were among those whose beliefs opposed war or bearing arms against other people.

Jehovah's Witnesses also experienced problems. Their religion teaches them to preach their faith actively. Some towns tried to pass laws limiting Jehovah's Witnesses' freedom to speak or pass out religious literature in public. During the 1900s, mobs disturbed their religious meetings, destroyed their kingdom halls—places of worship—and harassed them on the street.

Jehovah's Witnesses also believe that it is against God's law to worship a "graven image." Therefore, they do not salute the flag or recite the Pledge of Allegiance. During the 1930s, thousands of children were expelled from school for refusing to take part in required flag-salute exercises. They were called "unpatriotic."

In the 1930s and 1940s, Jehovah's Witnesses were punished for their religious beliefs.

The Barnette children, who were Jehovah's Witnesses, were among those expelled. In 1943, in the case of *West Virginia State Board of Education* v. *Barnette*, the U.S. Supreme Court ruled that laws forcing citizens to salute the flag are unconstitutional.

These events show that America has not always been free of religious conflicts. In recent years, U.S. courts have worked hard to clarify the First Amendment and promote religious equality for all.

• The U.S. Supreme Court has the final word in all legal matters concerning religion and the First Amendment.

Chapter 3

LIVING WITH OUR DIFFERENCES

Since the 1800s, the United States has become home to people who follow many different religions. Immigrants brought varied traditions with them. New religions, too, have gained members. Native Americans also have renewed appreciation for their ancient spiritual traditions.

Americans do not always agree about religious matters. When individuals or groups cannot resolve these disagreements, they may turn to courts of law. The U.S. Supreme Court has made many legal decisions about First Amendment issues. The struggle to define religious freedom and clarify the lines between religion and government goes on to this day.

Religious Worship and Public Schools

During the 1960s, the U.S. Supreme Court ruled that it was illegal for public schools to conduct any type of religious worship. This included religious instruction, school-sponsored prayers, and reciting Bible verses for purposes of worship.

Parents who objected had asked the courts to stop these practices. They believed that religious practices in public schools violated, or infringed on, the rights of those students who did not hold the same beliefs as the majority.

The Supreme Court agreed that such practices violate the Establishment Clause of the First Amendment. In making these decisions, the Court pointed out that schools are run by the government and paid for by the taxes of all citizens. In turn, laws say that all young people, of all faiths, must attend school. Therefore, the Supreme Court reasoned that schools should be run in a way that takes no position on religious issues.

In the 1962 case, *Engel* v. *Vitale*, the Supreme Court said that school officials should not tell students how or when to pray. The Court said that schools should avoid conflict by leaving religious practices to the home and to religious institutions. The court tried to balance the rights of the students who wished to pray with those who did not. It said that students could pray, silently, anytime. They were also free to pray at home, at their places of worship, and elsewhere.

In addition, some justices (judges) of the Supreme Court expressed concern that forcing religious practices on individuals can harm religion. In a 1963 case, Justice William Brennan said that such observances might become "empty...with little, if any, spiritual significance."

Many religious leaders agreed with these Supreme Court decisions. They said that it might be impossible to find a prayer that was acceptable to all people of different faiths. Such a prayer would probably not have much meaning, they believed. Some clergymen echoed the opinion of Roger Williams, who had said, "Forced worship is false worship."

Supreme Court Justice William Brennan opposed the practice of religion in schools.

An Ongoing Debate

The debate over school prayer has not ended. Many Americans disagree with the Supreme Court's decision in *Engel* v. *Vitale*. They want public schools to sponsor prayers. Some schools, especially in southern states, have ignored the 1962 decision. School officials continue to conduct prayers, often at the start of the school day and at sports events.

In the 1963 case of *Abington School District* v. *Schempp*, the Supreme Court said that public schools could not use Bible reading for religious purposes. The Court, however, went on to discuss ways in which religion can be part of the school day. Justice Tom Clark pointed out that schools should teach students about religion. They can discuss the history of religion in America and other lands and look at ways in which religions are alike and different. They can also study how religion has contributed to the arts, to charities, and to other parts of human life.

In 1985, the Supreme Court heard a school-prayer case again. An Alabama law set aside time for silent prayer in public schools. The Court found that the main purpose of this law was to sponsor religious activity. Though the schools were willing to excuse those who did not wish to take part, the Court said that this did not solve the problem. Justice Sandra Day O'Connor said that "excusing" students from prayer sent the message that they were outsiders, not "full members" of the community.

Some states have "moment-of-silence" laws. These laws allow for a brief quiet period at the start of the school day. The time can be used for prayer, if students wish. Or students may think quietly about something else. Supporters say this is a way to balance rights of all people. Congress has considered passing a moment-of-silence law for public schools. Several school-prayer bills were also proposed during the 1980s and 1990s.

Furthermore, in 1990, the Supreme Court said that student religious groups, such as Bible-study clubs, have an equal right to meet on school property after school hours. The Court stated that if schools allow other kinds of groups to meet, they must give this same right to religious clubs.

Justice Sandra Day O'Connor helped to define school-prayer issues in her 1985 opinion on silent prayer.

Conflicts Over Schoolbooks

For more than a century, many Americans have been concerned about the textbooks used in public schools. During the 1800s, many non-Protestants were upset when stories and passages from the Protestant Bible were used in public school texts. They believed that these materials went against their own religion. By the early 1900s, such materials had been taken out of most books.

Since the early 1900s, Americans have disagreed about whether or not students should study a scientific theory called evolution. This theory holds that all living things on earth developed gradually, over a period of billions of years and that humans evolved from a lower order of animals. Charles Darwin, a British scientist, developed this theory. Darwin had traveled around the world on a scientific voyage. While studying plants, animals and fossils, he noticed connections among them and ways in which they were similar.

The issue of prayer in schools continues to stir debate, even to this day.

When Darwin's landmark book *On the Origin of Species by Means of Natural Selection* was published in 1859, it caused a stir among scientists. Religious leaders joined the debate, since evolution disagreed with the Biblical account of creation. Some religious leaders accepted the new theory and said that evolution was the means God had used to create living things.

Other people strongly opposed the idea of evolution. Some Protestant leaders openly condemned evolution and urged people to accept everything written in the Bible as a fact. They asked for state laws that would ban teaching evolution in public schools. Several states passed such laws.

Attorney Clarence Darrow defended John Scopes during a famous trial about teaching evolution.

In 1925, a teacher named John Scopes was arrested in Tennessee for teaching his biology students about evolution. In a famous trial (called the "Scopes Monkey Trial"), Scopes was found guilty and fined $100. The state supreme court reversed this decision but it did not go to the U.S. Supreme Court.

Religious Freedom for Native Americans

Many times in the past, the U.S. government tried to stop Indians from practicing their ancient religions. Churches set up religious communities, called missions, near Indian lands and forced many Native Americans to become Christians. During the 1800s, when various tribes were being moved to live on reservations, Indian children were sent to boarding schools, sometimes by force. They were taught white customs, including Christian faiths.

By 1900, Native Americans had lost most of their homelands. On these lands were many sacred sites—springs, lakes, rocks, mountains, and other natural locations that are important in their religious traditions. The loss of these sites limited their freedom of worship.

Trying to right a past wrong, the U.S. government returned the sacred Blue Lake to the Taos Indians of New Mexico in 1970. Other tribes have also received certain lands back. Some are still working to have their sacred sites returned.

This historical photo, taken in the early 1900s, shows a group of Nez Percé in front of St. Joseph's Mission in Idaho.

In 1978, Congress passed the American Indian Religious Freedom Act. It protects the rights of native peoples in the United States to follow their traditional religions. It also gives protection to certain practices and to some cemeteries, sacred objects, and lands that are important to Indian religious traditions. Today, Native Americans are still struggling to gain the full religious freedom that was granted to others two centuries ago.

In 1968, the Supreme Court did hear a case about evolution law. An Arkansas teacher, Susan Epperson, was using a textbook that discussed Darwin's theories. The Court ruled that the anti-evolution law violated teachers' rights to free speech. It also said that the law violated the First Amendment ban against an "establishment of religion."

Still, people have continued to argue about teaching evolution in public schools. Opponents have worked hard through the years to keep evolution out of textbooks. Texas did not resolve the matter until the 1980s, when the state board of education decided that texts must include material on this scientific theory.

Some states passed laws ordering that if evolution were taught in science classes, the Bible version of creation must also be taught. These were called "equal-time" laws. In the 1987 case of *Edwards* v. *Aquillard*, the Supreme Court said that the equal-time law was illegal. The Court found that there was no scientific evidence for the Biblical account of creation, so these ideas could not be taught as science. They also said that the law was intended to promote a specific religious viewpoint.

People still disagree about whether students should learn about evolution, as well as about AIDS, sex education, and other controversial subjects. In some schools, people have removed library books that include subjects or words that offend them. Around the country, people have also opposed various books and teaching materials that go against their beliefs. Their actions have angered parents and others who do not want somebody else to say what everyone in a school may learn or read.

Religion and Politics

Religion has also played a role in America's political life through the years. The Constitution says that religious beliefs may not be used to keep a person out of public office. This guarantee is written in Article VI, which says: "No religious test shall ever be required as a qualification to any office or public trust under the United States. . . ."

Also, in 1961, the Supreme Court said that states may not require people to take oaths (vows) regarding a belief in God.

Despite these laws, the issue of religion has come up in different ways both in local and national elections. Negative attitudes about people from certain religions has prevented a number of candidates from being elected.

Before 1960, a Catholic had never been elected president. During his campaign, John F. Kennedy was asked many questions about his religion. He told voters that he valued religious freedom as set forth in the First Amendment. This reassured people who worried that a Catholic president might try to advance Catholicism and limit their religious freedom. Some had also feared a Catholic leader might follow directions from the pope in Rome. Once Kennedy was in office, Americans saw that his private religious beliefs did not affect their religious freedom.

Jerry Falwell became one of America's most prominent "Religious Right" leaders in the 1980s.

During the 1980s, religion and politics were often together in the news. A number of people who felt strongly about traditional Christian values became more prominent in politics. They became part of what is called the Religious Right, or Far Right. Many important leaders in these groups are clergymen. Members of the Religious Right have run for public office. Others have worked to help their candidates win local and national elections.

Critics believed some members of the Religious Right were mixing religion and politics in harmful ways. In 1984, critics objected when certain politicians called their opponents "ungodly." They opposed using political slogans like "Send another Christian to Congress" or "Take territory for our Lord, Jesus Christ." They said that voters should not be told to choose candidates on the basis of religion. They also said that candidates had no right to claim that God supported their bid for office or that non-Christians should never be elected.

Cults

In 1993, a tragedy in Waco, Texas, made news headlines around the nation. For years previous, federal officers had been investigating a small religious group called the Branch Davidians led by David Koresh. Koresh had been illegally stockpiling weapons. In February 1993, the Bureau of Alcohol, Tobacco, and Firearms (ATF), the federal agency that regulates the sale of weapons, planned to arrest David Koresh at the Davidian compound. Somehow the Branch Davidians found out that a raid was going to take place, and when officials attempted to arrest Koresh there was a shootout.

The Branch Davidians are a type of religious group called a cult. Cults are defined as groups of people who follow a leader who has founded a new religion. Cult leaders have typically been powerful people who insist that their followers obey them. Some cult leaders have told members to give all their money and possessions to the cult or told them whom to marry.

David Koresh had told his followers that they must collect arms to defend themselves against outsiders. He also told them that the end of the world was approaching and only his followers would be saved.

The number of cults in the United States began growing during the 1960s. Groups that are commonly called cults include the Unification Church (founded by Reverend Moon), Worldwide Church of God, the Divine Light Mission, and the Society for Krishna Consciousness (Hari Krishnas). By 1992, it was thought that between 400,000 and 3 million Americans belonged to cults.

Some people worry that certain cults are formed simply to take advantage of specific tax laws that make religious organizations exempt from paying taxes. The ways in which many cults go about raising money have also been questioned. Some cult leaders have even been charged with breaking labor laws.

What is a "real" religion? What groups should receive the tax benefits given to religious organizations? Which should not? Lawmakers continue to debate these questions.

• A Jewish scribe explains a passage from the Torah to two youngsters at New York's Temple Emanuel, the largest Jewish house of worship in the world.

PROTECTING THE FREEDOM TO WORSHIP

The United States today is quite different from what it was when the Bill of Rights was written and approved. In 1791, there were some 3 million Americans, mostly Protestants, living in 13 states and several territories. Today, 50 states stretch from coast to coast, north to Alaska and southwest to the Hawaiian islands. There are more than 280 million Americans. They may belong to one of nearly 2,000 different religious groups, or to none at all. Some of today's immigrants still come to America for religious freedom.

Respecting the Rights of Others

At times, newspapers or television news programs describe acts of intolerance or "hate speech" directed against people based on their religion. Such acts hurt people and keeps the nation from reaching its highest ideals of respect and equality for all.

Concerned by such events, some communities sponsor programs to help people get along better. They hope to increase people's respect for one another. Members of different religious groups often join together in educational programs and social activities.

Schools also sponsor education programs that encourage mutual respect. One program that has been used in

Mormons, shown in a Utah class, are one of America's many prominent faiths.

A Celebration of Religious Freedom

The Williamsburg Charter is a special document that was written in 1988. It celebrates religious liberty in America, and the freedoms set forth in the Bill of Rights. More than 200 well-known Americans from different walks of life worked together on the charter and signed it.

The charter admits that Americans have deep differences when it comes to religion. But it explains that there are certain principles that people can agree on. It says that religious liberty is a right. In a free society, people must respect the rights of minorities and of those with unpopular views, just as they respect the rights of the majority. The signers of the charter expressed their belief that "a right for one is a right for another and a responsibility for all."

many schools is called "A World of Difference." It began in Boston, Massachusetts, in 1985 and was developed by the Anti-Defamation League of the B'nai B'rith, a Jewish group. Several American companies have sponsored "A World of Difference." In the course, students learn about racism and religious intolerance in American life. Students discuss the various problems of segregation, separateness, violence toward minorities, and vandalism at places of worship. They also learn about ways to combat prejudice.

In addition, schools make adjustments for the differing beliefs of students. They may give students time off on important religious holidays. That way, they can attend services and celebrate with their families. Teachers may discuss what various holidays mean to the religious groups who celebrate them. In many schools, students perform songs from various religious traditions in their seasonal programs.

Individuals can do their part to support freedom of worship. We can understand what problems occur when religious intolerance is shown toward others. We can read about the struggle for religious freedom in early America and see why it meant so much to those who became Americans. We can treat other people with respect, as we would wish to be treated ourselves. We may also have opportunities to make friends with people of different beliefs and learn about their religious traditions.

A Gift to the World

The early leaders of America pictured a nation where religion was not controlled by rulers. Rather, it was left to the sense of right or wrong of each individual. Many early Americans viewed religion as an essential part of life. They thought that religious institutions could do much to meet people's spiritual, emotional, and physical needs. The people who wrote the Constitution, however, thought that religious freedom would best succeed if religion and government were kept separate.

Freedom to worship was one of the first freedoms that Americans could treasure. To some historians, religious liberty has been America's greatest gift to the world. Other countries have seen how the First Amendment to the Constitution allows Americans to follow their own beliefs. They have admired the idea of separating church and state.

Some countries have followed this example. They have given a written promise of liberty to their own citizens. They also have designed systems in which religion and government are separate.

The history of freedom of religion in America has not always been smooth. There have been conflicts, and some individuals and groups have been the victims of intolerance. Yet, the First Amendment guarantee has withstood the test of time. It continues to be respected and to guide the great American experiment in religious freedom.

Understanding the Bill of Rights

★ ★ ★ ★ ★ ★ ★ ★ ★ ★ ★ ★ ★ ★ ★ ★ ★ ★

In 1791, the Bill of Rights became part of the U.S. Constitution. What are these rights and why are they important for us?

The First Amendment says that the government cannot interfere with people's rights to freedom of speech, freedom of the press, freedom of religion, and freedom of assembly. It also gives people the right to petition their leaders.

The Second Amendment says because a "well-regulated militia" is "necessary to the security of a free state," the government can't interfere with the people's right to "keep and bear arms." Arms are guns and other weapons.

At the time the Bill of Rights was written, most men still belonged to their local state militia, or army. They kept their guns at home so they could be ready to defend their country at a moment's notice.

Some people say that because we have no such state militia today, the Second Amendment doesn't give people the right to own guns. But other people say that the Second Amendment guarantees the right to own guns for many purposes, including defense of home and family.

The Third Amendment says that, except in time of war, troops cannot be lodged in private homes without the permission of homeowners. This was included because many people remembered a time when the British had forced citizens to open their homes to soldiers.

The Fourth Amendment says that people's homes and possessions can't be searched or taken without an official paper called a *warrant*. A warrant is a document, signed by a judge, that allows police to search for evidence of a crime. The amendment also says that a warrant cannot be issued without "*probable cause*." This means that the police must convince a judge that the search of a specific place is likely to produce evidence of a crime.

The Fifth Amendment protects people who are accused of crimes. It says that for a serious crime, such as murder, a person must be charged with the crime by a group called a grand jury. Twelve to twenty-three people make up a grand jury. They must examine the evidence that the government has against the person and then determine whether there is a strong enough case to charge the person with a crime.

The Fifth Amendment also says that a person can't be tried twice for the same crime and doesn't have to testify against himself or herself. In a trial, when someone who is on trial refuses to answer questions on the witness stand, we say the witness "takes the fifth."

Another important part of the Fifth Amendment says that no person can be "deprived of life, liberty, or property, without due process of law." This part of the amendment guarantees all citizens the right to a fair trial before they can be executed, put in prison, or have property taken away from them. It also means that any laws made in the United States must result in fair treatment of all citizens.

Last, the Fifth Amendment says that the government can't take anyone's property for public use without paying a fair price for it.

The Sixth Amendment gives people who are accused of crimes the right to a speedy and public trial by a jury of people from the area where the crime was committed. Without the right to a speedy trial, people could be arrested for crimes and stay in jail for years without ever having the chance to defend themselves in court. The amendment also says that those accused of crimes have the right to know their accusers, to be confronted by the people who have accused them, and to have a lawyer defend them.

The Seventh Amendment gives people involved in lawsuits over money or property the right to trial by a jury. It also says that once a decision is made by that jury, the decision can't be changed unless it can be shown that the trial was flawed in some way.

The Eighth Amendment protects people who are put in jail. The first part of the amendment says that a judge cannot require "excessive bail" for someone accused of a crime. Bail is money that a person must pay to be freed from jail during the time before a trial begins. The money is returned after a person shows up for trial.

The Eighth Amendment also says that no one can be given "cruel and unusual punishment" for a crime. If a person were convicted of stealing a loaf of bread, for example, it would be cruel and unusual punishment to sentence that person to ten years in jail. The rule against cruel and unusual punishment also prevents such things as the torture of prisoners.

The Ninth Amendment says that the fact that some rights are not specifically mentioned does not mean that the people do not have them.

The Tenth Amendment says that any powers not given to the government by the Constitution belong to the states and the people. This amendment was very important to people at the time the Bill of Rights was ratified. Many people still feared a large, powerful national government, and this amendment put limits on the government.

The Bill of Rights gave citizens of the United States many freedoms and protections that few people in other parts of the world had.

Glossary

★ ★ ★ ★ ★ ★

Bill of Rights The first ten amendments to the United States Constitution, containing a list of the rights of citizens.

cult Members of an unusual or new religion directed by leaders who strongly control the group.

discrimination Favoring one group as opposed to another on the basis of their religion, race, gender, or nationality.

dissent To disagree or oppose.

diversity A variety; differences.

established religion A religion that is sponsored by the government and may also receive government aid.

Establishment Clause The first portion of the First Amendment, which forbids the government from establishing—setting up or sponsoring—a religion.

evolution A scientific theory saying that all living things on earth developed slowly over billions of years and that humans are related to a lower order of animals.

Free Exercise Clause That portion of the First Amendment that says the government shall not make any laws "prohibiting the free exercise" of religion.

heresy Speaking out against religious teachings, religious leaders, or a government-backed religion.

intolerance Disrespect toward different beliefs or ways of life.

Nativist movement Anti-immigration political group formed during the 1800s that tried to limit the rights of Catholics, Jews, and others.

persecution Harassment or mistreatment.

Religious Clauses Principles of religious freedom contained in the first sixteen words of the First Amendment in the Bill of Rights.

Religious tests Banned by the Constitution, these would require people to support certain religious beliefs in order to qualify for public jobs or public office.

Further Reading

★ ★ ★ ★ ★ ★ ★ ★ ★ ★ ★ ★

Colman, Warren. *The Bill of Rights*. Chicago: Children's Press, 1989.

Goldish, Meish. *Our Supreme Court*. Brookfield, CT: The Millbrook Press, 1994.

Greene, Carol. *The Supreme Court*. New York: Franklin Watts, 1981.

Johnson, Linda Carlson. *Our Constitution*. Brookfield, CT: The Millbrook Press, 1992.

King, David. *First Facts About U.S. History*. Woodbridge, CT: Blackbirch Press, 1996.

Rappaport, Doris. *Engel* v. *Vitale*. New York: HarperCollins, 1993.

Schleifer, Jay. *Our Declaration of Independence*. Brookfield, CT: The Millbrook Press, 1992.

Summer, Lila E. *The Judiciary: Laws We Live By*. Austin, TX: Raintree Steck-Vaughn, 1993.

Index

★ ★ ★ ★